How Food Is Made

LEVEL 9

Teaching Tips

Gold Level 9

This book focuses on developing reading independence, fluency, and comprehension.

Before Reading

- Ask readers what they think the book will be about based on the title. Have them support their answer.

Read the Book

- Encourage readers to read silently on their own.
- As readers encounter unfamiliar words, ask them to look for context clues to see if they can figure out what the words mean. Encourage them to locate boldfaced words in the glossary and ask questions to clarify the meaning of new vocabulary.
- Allow readers time to absorb the text and think about each chapter.
- Ask readers to write down any questions they have about the book's content.

After Reading

- Ask readers to summarize the book.
- Encourage them to point out anything they did not understand and ask questions.
- Ask readers to review the questions on page 23. Have them go back through the book to find answers. Have them write their answers on a separate sheet of paper.

© 2024 Booklife Publishing
This edition is published by arrangement with Booklife Publishing.

North American adaptations © 2024 Jump!
5357 Penn Avenue South
Minneapolis, MN 55419
www.jumplibrary.com

Decodables by Jump! are published by Jump! Library.
All rights reserved. No part of this book may be reproduced in any form without written permission from the publisher.

Library of Congress Cataloging-in-Publication Data is available at www.loc.gov or upon request from the publisher.

ISBN: 979-8-88996-921-1 (hardcover)
ISBN: 979-8-88996-922-8 (paperback)
ISBN: 979-8-88996-923-5 (ebook)

Photo Credits

Images are courtesy of Shutterstock.com. With thanks to Getty Images, Thinkstock Photo and iStockphoto. Cover – deryabinka. 4–5 – Elena Elisseeva, forden. 6–7 – Dan Su Sa, LilKar. 8–9 – Juice Flair, msheldrake, Yoyochow23. 10–11 – HandmadePictures, Ljupco Smokovski, M. Unal Ozmen, Chones, casanisa. 12–13 – Zigzag Mountain Art, J_K. 14–15 – Yatra4289, Bits And Splits, Matyas Rehak. 16–17 – Alter-ego, Ixepop. 18–19 – saiko3p, Volosina, photowind. 20–21 – ilkka Kukko, Lesya_boyko.

Table of Contents

From Field to Feast

Our food does not just appear on our plates. It has to be made. Food often starts its journey as a plant in a field.

Plants used for food are called crops.

We can eat some plants just as they were grown. But other plants need to go through extra steps on their way to our plates. How do we turn crops into foods we can eat?

The Path to Potatoes

From mashed potatoes to French fries, potatoes can be used in many different ways. Whichever potato is your favorite, they all start the same way. Potatoes are grown in the ground. First, a seed potato is planted.

Seed potato

Above the ground, potato plants grow leaves, but the new potatoes are hidden underground. Farmers pay close attention to the potato leaves. When the leaves turn yellow, that means it is time to dig up the potatoes.

Some potatoes are sold at **farmers markets**. Other potatoes are sent to factories to be cleaned and **packaged** before they are ready to be sold in stores. Some potatoes are sent to different factories where they are used to make something else.

Potatoes can be made into many different foods. Hash browns and potato chips are two. There are plenty of ways to cook fresh potatoes too, such as baking, **roasting**, or boiling them.

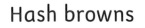

Hash browns

The Beginning of Bread

Bread is eaten all over the world. It can come in many different shapes, sizes, and **flavors**. Most bread is made using the same basic ingredients. These are flour, water, **yeast**, and salt.

First, these ingredients are mixed together and made into a stretchy ball of dough. This dough is pressed, folded, and stretched. This is called kneading. After it has been kneaded, the bread is left to rest. This helps it rise.

Bread dough can be cooked in lots of different ways. The way it is cooked depends on the type of bread that is being made. For instance, bagels are boiled in water before being baked in an oven.

Some bakers add other ingredients to their bread, such as fruits, cheese, and olives. Bread can be made into different shapes, such as baguettes or rolls. Bread dough can even be made to use in other foods, such as pizzas.

The Story of Sugar

Sugar is grown on farms in lots of different countries around the world. We get sugar from two plants called sugarcane and sugar beets. They are very different plants, but the sugar inside is exactly the same.

Sugarcane

Sugar beet

Factories turn sugar beets and sugarcane into sugar. The plants are cut into tiny pieces. These pieces are crushed until they make a sugary juice. The juice is boiled and turned into syrup.

As the syrup cools down, tiny sugar crystals form. These crystals are cleaned and packaged. They are sold as sugar! It is thought that people have been using sugar for around 10,000 years. It has many different uses.

Some sugar is sold in stores. People use it to bake cakes and cookies. Other sugar is turned into something else before it is sold in stores. Some sugar is boiled and stretched into shapes to make candy.

The Course of Chocolate

Chocolate is made from cocoa beans. These beans are found inside cocoa pods, which grow on trees. Once they have been taken out of the pods, the beans are dried by a machine or the sun.

Cocoa pods

Cocoa beans

Once the beans are dried, they go to a factory. There, the beans are cleaned and roasted to bring out the delicious chocolate flavor. The beans are then ground up. This turns them into a thick brown liquid called cocoa mass.

Once the cocoa mass has been made, other ingredients might be added. These could include milk, fruits, or nuts. This mixture is put into another machine that makes it smooth.
The liquid chocolate is poured into **molds**.

Mold

The chocolate is cooled down so that it sets and becomes solid. The chocolate is put into its packaging and sent away to be sold. You can buy many different types of chocolate, such as milk chocolate and dark chocolate.

Index

bagels 12
cocoa beans 18–19
crystals 16
hash browns 9
leaves 7

How to Use an Index

An index helps us find information in a book. Each word has a set of page numbers. These page numbers are where you can find information about that word.

Page numbers

Example: balloons 5, 8–10, 19

Important word

This means page 8, page 10, and all the pages in between. Here, it means pages 8, 9, and 10.

Questions

1. How do farmers know when it is time to dig up potatoes?

2. What are the two plants we use to make sugar?

3. What ingredients might people add to chocolate?

4. Using the Table of Contents, can you find which page you can read about bread?

5. Using the Index, can you find a page in the book about hash browns?

6. Using the Glossary, can you define what farmers markets are?

Glossary

farmers markets:
Places where local farmers sell food.

flavors:
Tastes.

molds:
Containers with certain shapes that people pour liquid into.

packaged:
Put into a box or carton.

roasting:
A cooking method that uses dry heat to cook food.

yeast:
A fungus that makes bread dough rise and take shape.